PHILOST

HILDEGARD

PHILOSOPHERS OF THE SPIRIT

HILDEGARD

Edited by

Robert Van de Weyer

Hodder & Stoughton
LONDON SYDNEY AUCKLAND

Copyright © 1997 Robert Van de Weyer

First published in Great Britain 1997.

The right of Robert Van de Weyer to be identified as the Editor of this
Work has been asserted by him in accordance with the
Copyright, Designs and Patents Act 1988.

1 3 5 7 9 10 8 6 4 2

All rights reserved. No part of this publication may be reproduced,
stored in a retrieval system, or transmitted, in any form or by any means
without the prior written permission of the publisher, nor be otherwise
circulated in any form of binding or cover other than that in which it
is published and without a similar condition being imposed on the
subsequent purchaser.

British Library Cataloguing in Publication Data:
A record for this book is available from the British Library.

ISBN 0 340 69402 5

Typeset in Monotype Columbus by
Strathmore Publishing Services, London N7.

Printed and bound in Great Britain by
Mackays of Chatham PLC, Chatham, Kent

Hodder and Stoughton Ltd,
A division of Hodder Headline PLC
338 Euston Road, London NW1 3BH

CONTENTS

The first task of philosophers is to ask questions – the questions which lurk in all our minds, but which, out of fear or confusion, we fail to articulate. Thus philosophers disturb us. The second task of philosophers is to try and answer the questions they have asked. But since their answers are inevitably only partial, philosophers both interest and infuriate us. Their third and most important task is to stimulate and inspire us to ask questions and seek answers for ourselves.

The human psyche or spirit has always been the main – although not the only – focus of philosophy. And inevitably when the psyche is explored, the gap between religion and philosophy rapidly narrows. Indeed for philosophers in the more distant past there was no gap at all, since philosophy was an aspect of theology and even mysticism. Although religious institutions are now quite weak, questions of spiritual philosophy are being asked more keenly and urgently than ever.

This series is an invitation to readers, with no philosophical training whatever, to grapple with the great philosophers of the spirit. Most philosophy nowadays is served in the form of brief summaries, written by commentators. Each of these books contains an introduction to the life and ideas of the philosopher in question. But thereafter the reader encounters the philosopher's original words – translated into modern English. Usually the words are easy to follow; sometimes they are more difficult. They are never dull, always challenging, and frequently entertaining.

INTRODUCTION

Hildegard was, and is, a powerful woman. In her own time she had the power both to disturb and to attract her contemporaries. And today, across eight centuries, she continues both to disturb and to attract those who read her writings, listen to her music – and through those two media, encounter her towering personality.

Her power derives in part from the sheer emotional and intellectual intensity of all that she did. From childhood onwards she had visions, which she believed were sent from God; and these visions are the basis of her writings. They are rarely peaceful, and more usually are both beautiful and frightening. Wild animals, men and women with glowing skin and strangely-coloured robes, castles decked with jewels, monsters with fire coming from every orifice, pregnant mothers with full-grown men in their wombs – these are the kind of images that fill her visions. She then sets about interpreting what she has heard and seen, giving philosophical and moral significance to every detail. And her interpretations display a mind of rare intelligence and originality.

This originality is the second source of her power – and is the reason why in recent decades interest in her work has burgeoned. Christianity over the centuries has had a rather negative attitude towards the material world, seeing it mainly as a source of temptation; the sole positive purpose of animals and plants is to provide food for human beings, who were seen as the summit of creation. Hildegard was one of the few Christian writers in the medieval period who rejected this attitude, putting forward a quite different theology. In her view the Word of God is present in every living creature, and is expressed in their beauty; thus the whole of God's creation should be cherished for its own sake. Even more remarkably, Hildegard seems at times to regard humankind not as the dominant species for whom other species exist to serve, but rather as the species called by God to serve all others. She believes that God has implanted a particular quality of wisdom in human beings, which enables them to perceive God's Word in themselves and in other creatures, and which therefore prompts them deliberately to care for the needs of all creatures.

The third source of Hildegard's power is her conviction of the spiritual equality of men and women – and her willingness to put that conviction into practice. The equality of the sexes is not a theme in her writings, but in her middle years it became a major aspect of her conduct. Despite fierce male opposition, and despite also the complacency of her fellow nuns, she wrested control of her convent from the control of the monastery in whose grounds it had developed. Later she discovered within herself a gift for public speaking; and in an age when preaching was entirely the preserve of priests and monks, she embarked on four extensive tours, giving sermons in cathedrals and churches throughout the German-speaking lands. To her own astonishment, men flocked to hear her. And without doubt she made it possible for other women of spiritual insight to gain respect in later decades and centuries.

She became without doubt the most famous woman of her day. And many sought her personal advice and counsel, recognising her profound insight into the human soul. This insight is the fourth and deepest source of her power. She possessed a remarkable ability to understand the experiences of others, even those that she herself could not have shared; she even writes with vivid frankness about sexual intercourse. And her philosophical reflections are not merely the fruit of high intelligence; they are firmly rooted in the struggle for inner harmony and peace. As a result she is able to discuss human sin and wickedness without sounding judgmental, but with sympathy and understanding. She does not mince her words; but she knows that most sinful actions arise from lack of wisdom, rather than deliberate malice – and that the worst victims are usually the sinners themselves.

* * *

Hildegard was born in 1098 in Bermersheim, near the town of Alzay. She was the tenth and last child of a wealthy and well-connected family, which owned substantial estates. Her parents were devout, and two of her brothers became priests, while a sister became a nun. She started having visions when she was barely able to talk, and she wrote later that the ability to receive visions from God had been implanted in her while still in her mother's womb. She probably told her parents about these early visions, because when she was aged eight they decided to offer her as an oblate to the nearby monastery of Disibodenburg. This meant that she lived from that time onwards entirely within the monastic enclosure, participating fully in the rigorous routine of worship and study.

When she arrived the monastery was entirely male, except for an anchoress called Jutta, who lived in a small cell attached to the church. Hildegard was put under Jutta's care, living in an adjoining cell. The cells had small windows looking into the church, which enabled Jutta and Hildegard to join in the worship without mixing with the monks. As an anchoress Jutta spent many additional hours each day in silent meditation, praying for the monks and for the needs

of the wider world. Jutta thus had little time to edu-
cate her young charge; moreover, according to
Hildegard's later testimony, Jutta herself had received
little education in her youth. Hildegard responded by
ordering books from the monastery library, and the
hours that Jutta devoted to silent prayer Hildegard
spent reading. Hildegard emerged into adulthood
with a wide knowledge of philosophy and theology
which impressed all who met her, and the lack of
external guidance allowed her own imagination and
intellect to flourish freely.

Through the years of Hildegard's childhood
Jutta's reputation for sanctity spread, and other
women came to join her. Other cells were quickly
added until an entirely new cloister had been built. At
the age of fifteen Hildegard herself took the habit of
a nun. This spontaneous community of women
decided to constitute themselves as a Benedictine
convent, and elected Jutta as their first abbess. In 1136
Jutta died, and the nuns elected Hildegard as her suc-
cessor. Since the convent had developed out of an
existing monastery, the monks continued to administer it, taking any donations that were made to it; and
they expected the nuns to perform various chores for
them. The monks also regarded themselves as responsible for the spiritual welfare of the nuns, and
appointed one of their number as provost to fulfil this
duty. Hildegard decided that the nuns were now

ready to administer their own affairs, and decide for
themselves who should give them spiritual guidance.
The provost, a monk called Volmar, had become a
close friend, and supported Hildegard's wishes. But
they were unable to persuade the abbot or the other
monks to allow the nuns even the smallest degree of
independence.

In 1141 Hildegard came to believe that God
wanted her to disclose her visions. Some years earlier
she had told Jutta of her visions, who in turn had
alerted Volmar. Jutta may well have been sceptical,
and gave no encouragement to Hildegard to share her
visions more widely. But Volmar now offered to help
Hildegard describe her visions in writing. Hildegard
agreed; and with Volmar's assistance she composed
her first and greatest book, *Scivias*. The process took
several years, during which Volmar became utterly
convinced that the visions were genuinely divine in
origin. He persuaded the abbot of this, showing him
some of the early chapters. The abbot contacted the
Archbishop of Mainz, who sent the early chapters to
the pope. At the pope's insistence the chapters were
read aloud at a synod of bishops in Trier, who greeted
them with enthusiasm. Thus even before the book
was finished, it was being heralded as a work of mystical genius.

Until this time Hildegard had never doubted that
her visions came from God. But as her fame spread,

she became racked with doubt. Her anxiety that she might be exposed as a fraud grew so great that she fell ill, and was confined to bed. In 1145 she saw in one of the visions Bernard of Clairvaux, the most famous and revered mystical writer of the period. Two years later, as she lay in her cell unable to lift her head, she dictated a letter to him, asking for his approval in making her visions public. Bernard replied, assuring her that her visions were genuine, and urging her to finish her book quickly, so that others could benefit from what God had given her. On receiving Bernard's letter, Hildegard's illness faded, and she was restored to strength.

At first the monks of Disibodenburg were delighted at Hildegard's fame. The reputation of their monastery was hugely enhanced, attracting more visitors and greater donations. Her fame also induced the daughters and widows of many rich families to join Hildegard's cloister, bringing with them substantial dowries which further augmented the monastery's wealth. Hildegard, however, reacted quite differently, resenting even more strongly the monks' domination. She announced that she had been told in a vision that she and her sisters should leave Disibodenburg to found a new community elsewhere. She enlisted the support of the Archbishop of Mainz, and also a local aristocrat, the mother of one of her nuns, who set about looking for a site. But the abbot of Disibodenburg, who had been one of the first to acknowledge Hildegard's visions as genuine, was sceptical about this latest spiritual instruction; and he, along with the other monks, were anxious about the threat it posed to their material well-being. The monks may have had a part in stirring up local opposition: people in the neighbourhood publicly accused her of being mad, and of falsifying her visions for her own purposes. But Hildegard's most stubborn opponents were the nuns themselves, most of whom were quite content to be ruled by the monks.

Hildegard responded by falling ill again. For many weeks she lay on her bed, unable to move or speak. The abbot at first ignored her, assuming that her illness was a nervous reaction which would soon pass. But eventually he became anxious that she would die, and he decided to visit her. And when he saw her state, he concluded that her illness was a divine judgment on himself. He gave Hildegard and her community permission to move. Hildegard rapidly recovered. By then a site had been found for the new convent at Rupertsburg, about twenty miles away, and she arranged for a temporary chapel and cells to be built there. In 1150 she and a group of twenty nuns took up residence. There followed a long dispute with the abbot of Disibodenburg over the nuns' dowries which he wanted to retain; and this was only resolved in 1158 by a charter issued by the Archbishop of Mainz, which stipulated how the dowries should be divided.

Soon after the move to Rupertsburg an incident occurred which revealed an unpleasant side to Hildegard's character. From the time when she had first begun to disclose her visions, her strongest supporter within her community had been a cousin of Jutta, called Richardis. The mother of Richardis had helped found the new site at Rupertsburg, and Richardis had stoutly defended Hildegard against her opponents. In 1151 Richardis was invited to become abbess of another convent at Bessum; and after much prayer she accepted. Far from congratulating her, Hildegard was furious at Richardis' decision, accusing her of abandoning her true vocation for the sake of high office. Hildegard urged the nuns at Bessum to withdraw their invitation, portraying Richardis as unworthy of the role of abbess. The nuns were unmoved. And after Richardis arrived at Bessum, Hildegard wrote to her, saying that she was guilty of betraying their friendship, and that she should repent at once. Richardis became ill and died a few months later.

Despite these conflicts Hildegard's reputation as a visionary continued to grow, and the visitors and donations which formerly had come to Disibodenburg now came in even larger quantities to

Rupertsburg. Thus the temporary buildings were quickly replaced by magnificent stone structures. Hildegard increased her fame by writing two scientific works, the first of which was a study of the natural world, and the second a medical handbook analysing the causes, and proposing cures, for a wide range of conditions. She also wrote a second visionary work, *The Book of Life's Merits*, which explores human vices and virtues. Then in 1159, at the age of sixty, she set off on the first of her four preaching tours – the last of which was in 1170. The novelty of a female preacher, combined with her reputation, were themselves sufficient to draw large crowds. But the substance and style of her sermons also proved compelling, as she conveyed the beauty and the meaning of her visions in the language of the common people.

The move to Rupertsburg meant that Hildegard and her sisters were now responsible for conducting their own worship. Not content with simply reciting the divine office, Hildegard composed over seventy devotional songs for her community to sing. Using monastic plainsong as its basis, her music is astonishingly free, weaving different melodies to produce wonderful harmonies. In 1163, after her third preaching tour, she embarked on her final visionary text, *The Book of Divine Works*. It lacks the emotional intensity of *Scivias*, but possesses greater theological clarity.

The central part is a long meditation on the Word of God, based on the opening verses of St John's Gospel. In it she shows that her belief in the presence of God in all living things is firmly rooted in Scripture.

By 1165 the number of women wanting to become nuns under Hildegard's direction was so great that the buildings at Rupertsburg could no longer house them. So she founded a second convent near to Bingen. Despite her age she visited the new convent twice a week, which involved crossing the Rhine. She also welcomed large numbers of people seeking her help; and to her reputation as a mystic, preacher and musician she added that of a healer, curing both physical and mental illnesses.

The last five years of her life were clouded by two disputes. The first was with the monks at Disibodenburg. Under the resolution which had secured the independence of her community, the abbot of Disibodenburg was committed to supplying a monk of the nuns' choice to act as their chaplain. In 1174 Hildegard requested a monk called Godfrey, but the abbot sent another monk. Hildegard was incensed, and eventually referred the matter to the pope. The pope took Hildegard's side. Happily Godfrey immediately began to write a biography of Hildegard, which is the source of much of our knowledge about her.

The second dispute shows that her moral courage was undimmed by age. A local nobleman had been excommunicated from the Church, for reasons that Hildegard regarded as unjust. When he died Hildegard allowed his body to be buried in the convent cemetery. The archbishop of Mainz, one of Hildegard's strongest supporters, was away in Rome, and his subordinates responded to Hildegard's action by imposing an interdict on her convent, which prevented the nuns from receiving the sacraments. The interdict remained in force for several months until March 1179, when the archbishop returned.

Hildegard died six months later on 17 September. She has never formally been canonised, but the Church in Germany has long celebrated her sanctity on the anniversary of her death.

* * *

The heart of Hildegard's philosophy is her understanding of God's Word. From the opening verses of St John's Gospel she derives the notion that Logos – the Word of God – is the agent of all creation, and is thus present in every living thing, and indeed in every material object. Thus when she looks at an animal or plant, or even a clod of earth, she sees an embodiment of God's power and love. She retains the conventional distinction between the spiritual and material realms. But unlike most of her contemporaries – and, indeed, most religious people down the ages – she perceives a fundamental harmony between the two: the material realm is an expression and reflection of the spiritual.

Within the created order, humanity possesses one distinctive attribute, according to Hildegard: the faculty of wisdom. This faculty enables human beings to reflect upon the objects they see with their senses, and also to reflect upon themselves. Thus, while other living creatures are unconsciously animated by God's Word, human beings are aware of God's hand within and around them. This gives human beings moral freedom: they may choose to co-operate with God's Word, and so cherish and enhance the created order; or they may choose to defy God's Word, and thence hurt and damage the creation.

This choice between creation and destruction is, in Hildegard's view, exceedingly tough. She believes that human beings have an innate tendency to destroy what God has created; so they can only truly co-operate with God's Word if they undergo a mental, emotional and moral conversion. They must keep a constant watch over their patterns of thought and feeling, and over their habits of behaviour. And through this vigilance they become participants in an unceasing drama, in which sin and virtue – the urge to destroy, and the desire to create – fight one another for dominance. Indeed, in the final chapter of

Scivias the conflict between virtue and sin is actually presented in dramatic form.

Hildegard was not a systematic philosopher or theologian; her ideas and insights come almost randomly in her writings. And her prose is so convoluted and repetitive that it is often quite hard to discern those ideas and insights. Moreover, most modern readers will be less inclined than her contemporaries to accept that her visions come directly from God. For all these reasons her books are never likely to be as widely read as they were when they first appeared. Nonetheless she is rightly regarded by a growing number of people as a prophet for our times. By equating sin with the destruction of the world God has created, and by analysing how that destructive force within human beings can be overcome, she offers the foundation for a modern morality. And by unifying the spiritual and material realms within the ancient and Scriptural concept of Logos, she propounds a theology which can stir and inspire those who want to embrace that morality.

The present collection of Hildegard's writings is drawn primarily from *Scivias*, but also from her other major works. The extracts are grouped under broad themes, in an attempt to elucidate the underlying structure of her thought. As one reads these extracts one can understand why, as with her music, her writings were ignored during the eight centuries that separate her time from ours; they do not seem to speak to the needs and issues of the intervening period. Yet equally, like her music, her writings speak so forcefully to our own condition and culture that they seem almost as if they were written today.

ROBERT VAN DE WEYER

I
GOD AND WORD

———◆———

The Word of God showed the power of God by creating the world. The Word called into being from nothing all the different species which inhabit the world. These species all shine with beauty, reflecting the beauty of their origins. They sparkle in the beauty of their perfection, as if they have all been made of burnished copper. Their light shines in every direction, so the whole earth glows with beauty.

— SC 2.1.6

At the moment of creation God sent forth the brightest of all lights, his Word. God was not separate from the Word, just as a light is not separate from its source. Then in the person of Christ he sent the Word again. This time the Word was like a great fountain from which every person could drink, and never again be thirsty. Thus in the brightness of creation the mighty will of God was revealed. And in the coming of Christ, the love and wisdom of God was made manifest.

— SC 2.1.11

How is it possible that the Word of God could be made flesh in Christ, and yet not be separated from God? When the Word was being brought into the world through a human mother, the Word was simultaneously appearing in heaven, inspiring the angels to dance and rejoice, singing the sweetest praise of God. The Word entered time, without any stain of sin, and sent forth the light of wisdom to all who lived in the darkness of ignorance.

— SC 2.1.13

God is shown through the Word; the Word is shown through the creation of the world and all the species which inhabit it; and the Holy Spirit is shown through the Word being made flesh. What does this mean? God is the one who brought the Word into being before the beginning of time. The Word is the one through whom all creatures are made. The Holy Spirit is the one who enters creation at particular moments.

— SC 2.2.2

The Word of God is the deepest and sweetest love.

— SC 2.2.4

Salvation through love did not originate with us. On our own we do not know how to love, nor do we have the courage to choose love. Since the creator loved people so much, he sent his Word, in order to save us. The Word washes and dries the spiritual wounds we have inflicted on ourselves through sin. The Word washes us with his own sweat; from his skin the water of love flows.

— SC 2.2.4

Embrace God in the prime of your life, when you are vigorous.

— SC 2.2.9

The loving actions of Christ constantly shine before the soul. Some people feel diminished by the example of Christ, because they do not want to follow that example. Others feel uplifted; the light of Christ's love is for them an everlasting dawn. And they know that this light can never leave them.

— SC 2.6.13

When you see God's beauty, you are not looking with mortal eyes, but with the eyes of the soul. When you hear his Word, you are not using mortal ears, but listening with the ears of your soul to the wisdom he has implanted within you.

— SC 2.6.19

The Word of God is burning love. The Word brings life to those who are dead in soul. The Word is a light which exposes sin, and a flame which burns the ropes that bind sin to the soul. The Word exists in every person before the person is aware of the Word. The Word is the source of holiness in each person, and makes people desire to become holy. The Word is magnificent and glorious, and can never be comprehended by the human intellect.

— SC 3 *Introduction*

Imagine the highest and widest mountain in the world. Its size reflects the grandeur of God, and thus honours God. It is not greater than God; nothing on earth is greater than its creator. God is higher and wider than the human mind can comprehend. He is holier than we could possibly understand. No creatures can attain the holiness of God, because the holiness of God is above all creatures. Yet human beings, alone amongst the creatures on earth, are reluctant to honour God. They claim that it is difficult and tedious to worship God; they feel too weak to praise him. Every human being is a rebel against God.

— SC 3.1.1

God works through the Word. The Word has always been with God, sharing his glory. God ordered that the world be created, and the Word fulfilled his order. Every event has been planned by God from the beginning, and accomplished through the Word.

— SC 3.1.9

What sight in nature most faithfully reflects the Word of God? It is the sun rising above the horizon on a clear morning.

— SC 3.1.9

The kiss of eternal life, and the warm embrace of God's Word, are so sweet, and bring such pleasure, that you can never become bored with them; you always want more.

— SC 3.3 *Introduction*

The Word of God always reaches out to strangers, to the needy, to the poor and the weak, and to all those in pain.

— SC 3.3 *Introduction*

A human being cannot see and enter the full brightness of God. Humans can only see God through a dense cloud, which shields their spiritual eyes. So do not presume that you know God and understand him. Whenever you speak of God, tremble with uncertainty.

— SC 3.4.14

God does not need our praises. He cannot be moved by flattery. Soft-tongued sermons do not impress him. He sees the reality of our thoughts and actions, and judges us accordingly.

— SC 3.5.9

God uses his power sparingly and with compassion. He does not strike down sinners; he does not prune humanity of its evil branches. He waits with great patience for people to repent.

— SC 3.5.11

True knowledge exists within a human being like the reflection in a mirror, with God as the image being reflected.

— SC 3.5.30

Those who love God open themselves entirely to him. They ask him to enter their senses, their souls, and their minds. They receive him with joy; they embrace him with every thought and feeling; they want to perceive him with all their senses. And God rejoices in them, regarding them as more fragrant than the most fragrant flower in creation, as brighter than the brightest jewel, as nobler than the noblest mountain. And he wants to make them even sweeter in smell, even more sparkling, and yet more hand-some. He feasts their minds with delicious thoughts, and he presses his justice into their hearts. He gives them the sweetest spiritual water to refresh their souls. Yet sometimes he seems to abandon them, so that they find themselves without his help. He does this so that they do not become puffed up with spir-itual pride. They weep and moan, and may even become angry with God. In this way their faith is tested. In truth he does not leave them; his hand is still holding them. By stripping all vestiges of pride from them, the full extent of their goodness becomes manifest; and this enables their goodness to bear even greater fruit.

– SC 3.8.8

Think how much toil and sweat it takes to prepare a
field for sowing with seed. But once you have sown
the seed, it brings forth its harvest without further
effort on your part. Consider why this happens. It is
because God pleads with the earth to be fruitful. And
when the earth accepts his pleas, it provides you with
more food than you could possibly eat. But if God
does not plead with the earth, its fruitfulness is
reduced. As a result hunger may threaten your life.
Your relationship with God is similar. People are like
earth. If they receive the seed of God's Word with a
good heart, they bring forth a rich harvest of spiritual
gifts. But if they are reluctant to receive God's Word,
and even refuse to receive it, then they become spiritually dry, and the harvest is scarce.

— SC 3.10.4

Your eyes are not strong enough to look at God. Your
mind is not strong enough to comprehend his mys-
teries. You can only see and know what God allows.
Yet in your desire to see and know more, you engage
in all manner of foolish speculations, which cause
your soul to stagger. Just as water is absorbed by the
heat of a burning forge, so your soul is absorbed by
the restlessness of your thoughts, as you try to grasp
what is beyond your grasp.

— SC 3.10.5

Many people want to enjoy a good relationship with God, without making any mental and spiritual effort. To them religion is an enjoyable game. They do not try to achieve harmony with other people, or within their souls.

— SC 3.10.6

The Word of God regulates the movements of the sun, the moon and the stars. The Word of God gives the light which shines from the heavenly bodies. He makes the wind blow, the rivers run and the rain fall. He makes trees burst into blossom, and the crops bring forth the harvest.

— DW 1.2

The sky above us imitates God. Just as the sky has no beginning and no end, so God has no beginning and end. Just as the stars sparkle, so spiritual stars emanate from the throne of God, to sparkle within people's souls.

— DW 4.11

How could God be known, except through the living things which reflect his glory? How could we praise God, unless we had been created by him to sing his praises?

— DW 4.11

The Word of God spoke, and brought all creatures into being. God and his Word are one. As the Word spoke, so God's eternal will was fulfilled. The echo of the Word awakened life from inanimate dust.

— DW 4.105

When the Word of God spoke at the moment of creation, his sound was implanted in every creature, and gave life to every creature.

— DW 4.105

The love of God is symbolised by a leaping fountain. All who come near to it are showered by its sparkling waters. And they can see their own image in the pool below.

— DW 8.2

Everything lives in God, and hence nothing can truly die, since God is life itself. God is the wisdom that brought all things into being. He breathes life into all things.

— P 743 D

In all creation — in trees, plants, animals and stones — there are hidden secret powers which no one can discern unless they are revealed by God.

— P 893 C

God the Father is brightness, and that brightness is brilliant beyond our imagination. Many people try to separate God from his brightness. They see his brightness all around them in the beauty of his creation, but they do not ascribe this beauty to him. This brightness is the Father's love. All things are brought into existence through his love, and we are surrounded by his love.

— Letter to Bishop Eberhard

The Father designed the universe, the Son erected this design. The Father decided how the universe should be, and the Son carried out his orders. The light that illuminates God's creation, enabling us to see its beauty, is part of the life which existed before the creation, which has been in existence since before time. In fact this light does not merely illuminate creation, it is the energy through which all things come into being.

— Letter to Bishop Eberhard

2

CREATION AND FULFILMENT

———— ✦ ————

Search for God in everyone, since all people are
reflections of God. Search for God in everything,
since all creatures and objects on earth are made by
God. — SC 1.2.29

Use all your faculties to appreciate God's creation.
Use your soul to understand other souls. Use your
body to sympathise with other people's bodily expe-
rience. Use your emotions of anger and revenge to
understand war. Appreciate goodness through distinguishing it from evil. Appreciate beauty through distinguishing it from ugliness and deformity. Define
poverty by contrasting it with wealth. Rejoice in
good health by comparing it with sickness.
Distinguish the various opposites: length and short-
ness; hardness and softness; depth and shallowness;
light and darkness. Enjoy every moment of life by
constantly reminding yourself of the imminence of
death. Look forward to paradise by reminding yourself of eternal punishment. You understand so little of
what is around you because you do not use what is
within you. — SC 1.2.29

Do not mock anything that God has created. All creation is simple, plain and good. And God is present throughout his creation. Why do you ever consider things beneath your notice? God's justice is to be found in every detail of what he has made. The human race alone is capable of injustice. Human beings alone are capable of disobeying God's laws, because they try to be wiser than God.   — sc 1.2.29

The power of God is known through all the various species of plant and animal in the world, which have been created by the Word of God. As the power and honour of a person is known through the value of that person's word, so the holiness and goodness of the creator is known through the value of the creator's Word. And that value is made manifest through the creation.   — sc 2.1.4

A word which is spoken has three elements: sound, goodness, and breathing. A word has sound in order to be heard; goodness in order to be understood; and breathing in order that it may be completed. So too with God. The creation is God's sound, by which he enables all to perceive his power and glory. The coming of Christ is God's goodness, which prompts him to become a human being. And the Holy Spirit is God's breathing, by which he enters all people.

— sc 2.2.7

Look at the variety of creatures on earth. That demonstrates the wonderful imagination of their creator.

— SC 2.6.3

God created all things, fashioning all things to reflect his glory. All creatures by their very nature worship God, honouring him as their creator. Even the stones under your feet worship God, for hidden within every stone is a divine spirit. The true purpose of every creature has been ordained by God.

— SC 3.1.1

God's work of creation is completed by humanity. Human beings are the agents of God, destined to fulfil his purposes according to his plans. Through the work of human beings the world will be made perfect, and the world will reflect back to God perfectly the light of his glory. The world will thus come to an end, although God himself has no end. God was, and is, and will be — from before the beginning of time, to beyond the end of time.

— SC 3.1.10

God does not make things better, because his creation is already perfect. He is like a flame which illuminates all things, revealing their perfect goodness.

— SC 3.1.12

The power of God is not easy to see or understand. It is hidden in small events; it is concealed in small changes in our thoughts and attitudes. Yet these small events and changes can have large consequences; and these consequences are often easy to see. Indeed our perception of God is like our perception of one another. One person cannot see directly the thoughts and intentions of another person. It is only the consequences of those thoughts and intentions – in their facial expressions and their actions – that are visible.

– SC 3.5.1

The rest of God's creation cries out against the evil and perversity of the human species. Other creatures fulfil the commandments of God; they honour his laws. And other creatures do not grumble and complain at those laws. But human beings rebel against those laws, defying them in word and action. And in doing so they inflict terrible cruelty on the rest of God's creation.

– SC 3.5.17

Throughout all eternity God wanted to create human beings, because he wanted partners in his task of creation.

– DW 1.2

The Word is at the service of all creatures; and all creatures reflect his radiance. The Word is the life that lasts forever; and all creatures are animated by this life.

— DW 1.2

If human beings abuse their position of power over the rest of God's creation, then God will allow other creatures to rise up and punish them. Do not regard other creatures as existing merely to serve your bodily needs. By cherishing them as God requires, your soul will benefit.

— DW 3.2

God performed his work of creation so well that no creature is imperfect. Every creature is perfect according to its own nature, able to act as God intended.

— DW 9.2

God cannot be seen, but he is known through his creation – just as a person's body cannot be seen, but its size and shape can be inferred from its clothing.

— DW 9.14

God created the world out of the four elements to glorify his name. He strengthened the world with the wind. He connected the world to the stars, whose light bestows wisdom on the world. And he filled the world with all kinds of creatures. He then put human beings throughout the world, giving them great power as stewards of all creation. Human beings cannot live without the rest of nature, so they must care for all natural things.

— P 755

Human beings stand at the centre of God's creation, since they have greater understanding than all the other creatures with whom they share the world. Although they are small in stature, human beings are powerful in spirit. While their feet are on the ground, their heads can attain great spiritual heights.

— P 761

When the elements from which the world is made work in harmony, the soil is health, the trees yield abundant fruit, the fields yield abundant harvests, and all are happy. But if the elements do not work in harmony, then the world becomes sick. The same applies to human beings. If the elements from which humans are made work in harmony, then the body and mind are healthy; but if they are disharmonious, the body and the mind become sick.

— CC 49, 40

3
SOUL AND BODY

———————•———————

Remember that you were made in the image of God.
So you should love yourself, recognising your own
beauty as a mirror of God's beauty. And you should
want to use your abilities in the service of others,
recognising that these abilities are gifts from God. Do
not be afraid of pain and suffering. Just as gold is
made pure by fire, and precious jewels made to shine
by polishing, so you must be refined and polished.
Just as refined gold and polished jewels perfectly
reflect the sun's rays, so you will perfectly reflect the
love of God.

— SC 1.2.29

There are three aspects to a human being: the soul,
the body, and the sense. These three must operate in
harmony to make the person strong. The soul gives
life to the body; and the body causes the senses to
work. The body, however, attracts the soul to itself;
and the soul understands what the senses perceive. In
this way the senses touch the soul. The soul is the
source of the will, by which it can cause the body to
act according to God's laws. — SC 1.4.18

The faculty of understanding has been attached to the soul just as the arms are attached to the body. Through the divine wisdom which the soul possesses, it can understand the difference between good and evil, distinguishing between those acts which are good and those which are evil. The soul is like the master of understanding. It can separate good from evil, as wheat is separated from chaff. It can investigate whether things are useful or useless, lovable or hateful, creative or destructive. Just as salt gives taste to food, so understanding gives power to the soul.

— SC 1.4.19

The will exercises great power. It resides in the soul, like a man residing in his house. He stands in one corner of the house, seeing everything, and giving orders as to what should be done. The will does the same thing, giving orders to the soul, which in turn determines how the body will act.

— SC 1.4.20

The will is like an oven, in which every action is cooked. We cook bread in an oven and then feed it to people, so they are strong and can work. We prepare our actions within the will, deciding what should be done; we then feed those decisions to the body.

— SC 1.4.21

Those who wish to know God, but do not have in their hearts the faith and hope that one day they shall know God, will remain in ignorance.

— SC 2.5.5

God is like a stone in every human being. Just as a stone is always true to itself, so is God. Just as a stone can never change its form or shape, so God can never change. Within every person God is true and unchanging.

— SC 3.1.12

You do not know how you were created. Yet now you presume to stand in judgment over God's creation, determining what is good and bad, what is high and low. Remember, you do not know how life came into your body; and you do not know how to live outside your body. God alone understands these things.

— SC 1.2.30

The moment of choice is like standing at a crossroads, and saying to yourself: 'I could go this way, or I could go that way.' One way leads upwards, the other downwards. The path going upwards, which will require the greatest effort, leads to beauty and goodness.

— SC 3.2.12

Once the faculty of reason has chosen that which is good, the faculty will put that choice into practice, causing the mind, body and limbs to move in the appropriate manner. The faculty of will has been given by God, as the channel of his grace; through the human will God enables people to act according to his will.

— SC 3.2.12

Look in a mirror, and ask yourself: 'Am I beautiful? Is there vitality in my face?' Look into your face, and discern within yourself the potential both for good and for evil, for beauty and for ugliness, for life and for death. See also that you possess the faculty of reason, which God has breathed into your soul. Through this faculty of reason you are able to control your attitudes and actions. The faculty of reason will never depart from you; it belongs to God, and thus exists for all eternity. Through reason you can constantly choose those attitudes and actions whose fruits are good and beautiful, and avoid those which bear bad and ugly fruit. God in his grace has always breathed the faculty of reason into human beings.

— SC 3.2.12

Once people have committed themselves in faith to God, they submit their wills to his. This process happens without effort, because the human will knows that it is inferior to the divine will. Following God's will is a cause of pleasure and joy; the soul which is submissive to God feels warm and safe.

— SC 3.8.8

Those who have faith in God, and who submit to his will, come to understand him. Gradually they learn to discern his plan in each situation; and as they grow in understanding, they grow in love also, taking pleasure in everything God does. At the same time they also come to understand other people better, discerning their thoughts and intentions. And they learn to distinguish between those who are worthy of love and encouragement, and those who should be thwarted.

— SC 3.8.8

God has imprinted on the soul of every human being the image of the world as he wants it to be.

— DW 1.2

The soul is the life-force of the body, just as moisture is the life-force of a plant. Moisture makes a plant grow and be fruitful; so the soul enables the body to behave as it should, and be virtuous.

— DW 4.21

The soul assists the flesh, and the flesh assists the soul. Every good work is performed by the soul and the flesh together. The soul is always happy to co-operate with the flesh in good works. But the flesh is often irked when cooperating with the soul. The soul then stoops to the level of the flesh to give encouragement, just as a mother stoops to her weeping child to give comfort. In this way the flesh continues to work with the soul. The flesh often commits minor sins, which the soul tolerates, because it does not want to oppress the flesh more than the flesh can bear.

— DW 4.24

Human beings are earthly because their flesh is earthly; they are heavenly because their souls can reach the heights of heaven.

— DW 4.99

4
WISDOM AND REASON

———————◆———————

Some people have no fear of God, and in their perverse madness they scorn him. They cannot bear to think that there is one more powerful than they are, who is strong enough to overcome them, and who has greater knowledge than they possess. Even to contemplate the strength and the wisdom of God disturbs their equanimity.

— SC 1.2.4

God has implanted in your heart his wisdom. So throw out of your heart everything that contradicts this wisdom. While unwisdom overwhelms wisdom, you are like a deep dark lake where true life cannot survive. When you have thrown out unwisdom, follow the path that leads to freedom. This means obeying the wisdom that already shines within you. And as you do so, your own soul will come to life.

— SC 1.4.12

The wisdom of God which he has implanted in every person brings great blessings, both spiritual and material. It brings prudence, discretion and sound judgment. It enables people to use their abilities to the full in the service of others. Evil cannot enter those who obey the inner wisdom.

— SC 1.4.13

In the spring, after the winter rains have fallen on the earth, warmth enters the air, bringing the earth to life. In the same way, after an infant has been conceived in a woman's womb, God's Spirit enters the womb, giving wisdom to the infant. This wisdom is the source of true life.

— SC 1.4.16

The wisdom of God implanted in every person gives innocence to the small child; it enables the young adult to be useful and efficient; and it enables the old person, whose body has become feeble, to be gentle and wise.

— SC 1.4.17

When people begin to become aware of God within themselves, they start to grow in wisdom. God enjoys conversing with human minds that have discovered him. He is touched by these conversations, just as a king is touched by the throne on which he sits. He does not depend on conversations with humans, and yet finds peace and satisfaction through them.

— SC 3.1.2

The wise person does not want to look God proudly in the face, but to touch God with inner devotion.

— SC 3.1.3

In his goodness God gave people the power of reason, and he put wisdom in their souls. The combination of reason and wisdom enables people to make a clear and rational choice, about whether to love and serve God, or whether to reject him. Yet if they look carefully at themselves, and recognise that God is the source of their reason and wisdom, then they will undoubtedly choose to love and serve God, honouring him in all their thoughts and actions.

— SC 3.4.15

Humanity stands in the middle of God's creation. Although small in stature, human beings are powerful because they possess wisdom.

— DW 2.15

The Word of God pours wisdom into the minds of humans; and by this wisdom they can discern the Word in and around themselves. This wisdom enables them to stunt the growth of vices, and nurture the growth of virtues. And as vice withers and virtue blossoms, the heart is filled with joy.

— DW 2.19

The souls of faithful people follow the Word of God along the path of truth; and as they walk, they climb from one virtue to the next.

— DW 2.19

5
VIRTUE AND GOODNESS

Virtue is like a warm garment in a cold world. It is the source of charm in a harsh world.

— SC 1.1.4

Sincerity is not enough; those who are sincere, and yet lukewarm in their hearts, are feeble and sleepy in their actions, insulting others instead of serving them. Let sincerity be combined with keen alertness.

— SC 1.1.5

Humility and charity are like soul and body; they need one another for strength. Humility is like a soul and charity is like a body; they cannot be separated, but must work together.

— SC 1.2.32

All virtue comes from the Word of God, and is a recognition of God's virtue.

— SC 2.1.5

If a herb does not form a flower, then it is less useful for medicinal purposes. In the same way, if people do not form virtues, they will be of less spiritual value to those around them, because they will not radiate God's love.

— SC 2.6.9

When a baby bird emerges from an egg, it is tiny; yet it has the same form as the adult bird it will become. A baby insect, emerging from an egg the size of a grain, is so small that the human eye can barely see it; yet it has the same serene form as the adult insect it will become. Similarly a person at the beginning of the spiritual journey may be very small in virtue, wisdom and insight; yet in every soul there is the form of virtue, wisdom and insight that is to be found in Christ himself.

— SC 2.6.16

Those who are simple, and in their simplicity obey God's laws, cannot easily be tricked or deceived into doing wrong.

— SC 2.7.2

The good works of good people cloak them in holiness. Their good works are like a thousand stars, twinkling in the darkness, and shedding light all around. Their good works are like a thousand birds that carry them on their wings up into the sky, enabling them to look down and feast their eyes on the beauty of God's creation.

— SC 2.7.6

Do not underestimate the power of good works. They are like fountains of pure water, which drown all that is evil around them.

— SC 2.7.13

Human beings are very frail. As they walk along the path of virtue, they are easily pulled to one side by temptation. Wise people are very cautious, always looking out for temptation and trying to avoid it; they are humble enough to recognise their own frailty. Wise people also seek out the company of others, so they can support one another as they walk.

— SC 3.2.5

Virtue is strongest in those who are swift in their response to evil; who are harsh and ruthless in trampling down the evil thoughts in their minds. Virtue is weak in those who are slow and sluggish in their response to evil; who have little passion for goodness, and thus tolerate evil thoughts in their minds.

— SC 3.4.13

Through virtuous thoughts and acts we begin to penetrate the mystery of God, because our thoughts and acts are reflections of his.

— SC 3.4.15

God sees everything you do. He sees the actions which are useful and fruitful, and those which are useless and fruitless. Nothing is hidden from his sight. God also understands the inner cause of all you do. He weighs your spirit. He knows when you have fallen for temptation, and when you have resisted temptation. God sends sorrow and miseries to test you; but he does not ask you to endure anything beyond your capacity. He perceives when you remain faithful to him, and when you run away. God wants you to cultivate him in your heart.

— SC 3.4.21

God does not ask people to be more virtuous than their spiritual capacity allows. His expectations of people are always realistic and just. And he does not want people to expect too much of themselves, because those who want to exceed their capacity for virtue are defying God's will. People should be virtuous according to their capacity; no more, and no less.

— SC 3.4.21

However far a person has wandered from the path of virtue, God is still calling that person back.

— SC 3.4.21

The good person responds to the evil actions of others with goodness. The evil person responds to the good actions of others with evil.

— SC 3.5.5

A good person is flexible – willing and able to bend towards every opportunity for serving others.

— SC 3.8.8

Those who are simple and straightforward in their ways of thinking do not cause sorrow to others.

— SC 3.6.29

6

JUSTICE AND FREEDOM

———————◆———————

People start by fearing God; and this fear leads them to understand the justice of God. Even though the human mind is dull, it can move from fear to understanding through rational thoughts and investigation.

— SC 1.1.2

Those who seek to be poor in spirit may first be motivated by fear of God. They then discover that poverty of spirit frees them from the desire to boast and brag, and instead calms their minds and simplifies their lives. Thus the attitude of fear is changed into an attitude of grateful love. They no longer try to assert themselves, but to act with justice, following the footsteps of Christ. They become covered in the white tunic of purity.

— SC 1.1.3

You are so weighed down with the heaviness of your bodily needs and passions, that you do not see the glory that God has prepared for you. He wants you to enjoy the fullness of his justice. And he wants you to be so secure in his justice that no power can dislodge you from it. When God fashioned the fabric of this world, he planned that all humanity should live in perfect justice. So compare the injustice of your present life with the justice of God.

— SC 1.2.31

Why do you not look at God's love, which could set you free? Why do you not notice the good things which God is doing for you? Why do you not pay attention when God calls you back from spiritual death? Why do you prefer death to life?

— SC 1.4.10

God looks upon you with great love and wants to clasp you to his bosom, embracing you sweetly. Yet now you reject this love. You refuse to hear about the justice which God can bring, and the happiness which derives from this justice. If you yourself acted justly, you would not reject God's justice; you would rejoice in it.

— SC 1.4.10

The Church fulfils its purpose through all its members, and through their relationship with one another. If kings, dukes, rich merchants, poor workers and beggars are all able to talk freely with one another, then the Church is truly glorious. Under God's law all are equal; and all must obey with humility and devotion if they are to be saved. All are obliged to fast, to control their appetites, and perform good works. And all who obey God's law are loved by him with great intensity.

– SC 2.5.23

God shines with justice. He cannot be unjust. Sometimes in the name of justice, people do unjust things. They may be sincere in what they do, but are misguided by ignorance. This is unjust justice.

– SC 3.1.12

Fear, which causes the body to tremble, causes the soul to desire justice. This is because the soul fears the anger of God, which is provoked by injustice. So the soul can only assuage that fear by rejecting injustice and embracing justice. Embracing justice also causes the body to tremble. This is because the soul begins to burn with passion for justice.

– SC 3.5.31

The brightness of God shines in the good works of just people. Thus by responding with gratitude and joy to those good works, we are giving thanks and praise to God. And by participating in good works we are decorating his holy temple.

— SC 3.10.31

7

SIN AND REPENTANCE

———◆———

There are many who give the outward impression of being attentive to God, but are not willing to be moved by his guidance and his promptings. They delude themselves that they will be taken up to the highest place, and are entitled to the greatest blessings. In truth they shall be hurled down to the lowest place – with good reason.

— SC I.2.I

Those, who in the past have been thrown about by their sinful passions, need not despair. They should remember that there is time to change. They can throw themselves into the fountain of repentance. And let themselves be thrown about by its waters. They will be washed clean by their faults, and purified from their evil habits. The thick mud of sin in which their feet are caught will dissolve, and they will be able to lift themselves up. Their joyful angels will guide their steps towards God. They will come to understand Christ by imitating others.

— SC I.2.8

When human beings are free from the power of evil, God shines in them, and they shine with the light of God. They acquire on earth the brightness which they will have in heaven.

— SC 1.2.31

Who are you? You are dust made from dust. What did you know before you existed as a human being? You were born in misery and pain. And, left to yourself, you will die in misery and pain. Your life is an affront to the excellence of God; the injustice of your actions offends his perfect justice. Where is the source of the evil which rules your life? You are so puffed up with pride that you want to be above the stars, looking down on the creatures of earth — and even looking down on the angels. The angels obey the commandments of God, but you are too proud to obey anything but your own wishes.

— SC 1.4.10

People struggle both to be honest with themselves, and to deny the truth about themselves. Sometimes they succeed in being honest, and are able to confess their sins to God. Sometimes they are able to deny the truth about themselves, and so they cannot speak truthfully to God. Indeed those who deny the truth about themselves also want to deny the existence of God.   — SC 1.6.4

God in his mercy remembered the greatest and most precious species in his creation, namely humanity, whom he formed from the slime of the earth, breathing life into it. When sin had driven out true life, God provided life only again. He did this through sending his Word in human flesh, whose presence hurled humanity into the depths of repentance.

— SC 2.2.4

We ask God according to his holiness to forgive us our sins. And since we are sinners, with much evil inside us, we ought also to forgive those who have sinned against us. We should not pursue those who have wronged us and harmed us. To do this would be a betrayal of God, who does not pursue us. We should not judge and condemn others, because God alone can judge and condemn. We can only expect God's mercy, if we show mercy to others.

— SC 2.6.18

The cause of sin is blindness to the beauty of God, and deafness to his loving Word.

— SC 2.6.19

Those who are sinful find that their friendships are fragile and easily broken; loneliness is their lot. But their loneliness need not be permanent. Repentance restores friendship; the sinner who repents is rewarded with the pleasures of companionship.

— SC 2.6.99

Evil does not corrupt the five senses. It corrupts the faculty of understanding which interprets what the senses perceive.

— SC 2.7.19

In the majority of people evil and goodness are mixed together in almost equal proportions. They fear God, and yet also are addicted to sin. God sends them many trials and hardships, in order to break their addiction. But so long as they possess their youthful vitality, they continue to indulge their sinful desire. They cling to those burning desires until the fire of desire is cooled by the passing years.

— SC 3.4.17

There are some people who enjoy greatly the pleasures of the flesh, and yet whose souls are sweet and innocent. They take delight in their bodies, and fall for every temptation to indulge themselves. But they are free from every kind of hatred and jealousy. God does not punish them by taking away their pleasures. Instead he sends them ample food to eat and wine to drink. Despite their weakness, he regards them as his own children.

— SC 3.4.20

There are a few people whose souls are completely filled with arrogance, bitterness, hatred and jealousy. They do not wish to endure any pain or injury. They are captivated by power and wealth, and destroy within themselves the spirit of virtue that impedes their pursuit of power and wealth. God may allow these people the power and wealth which they crave. But they derive no pleasure from their earthly possessions; inside their souls they are utterly miserable. Only when they connect this misery with their cravings can they begin to resolve their dilemma.

— SC 3.4.20

You need not possess your sins forever. You can give them back to God. If you are truly sorry for what you have done, he will take them back.

— SC 3.5.4

Since you are weak and frail, you will continue to sin.
But, if you will truly love God, the pleasure you
derive from sin will always be overlain with fear. And
this fear, which God himself has instilled, will help
you to overcome sin. To become completely cleansed
of sin takes many years. But those who do not love
God feel no fear when they sin. For this reason they
remain caught in the swamp of sin, and will never be
cleansed.

— SC 3.5.4

When people begin to sigh and weep over their sins,
then they become open to the grace of God. Instead
of fearing God, they begin to find comfort in him,
because they know that he can transform their souls.
They lift up their spiritual eyes to see God; they open
their spiritual ears to hear his words; they move their
spiritual tongues to praise him; they raise their spiritual hands to rejoice in him; and their spiritual feet
carry them towards him.

— SC 3.8.8

Sometimes God touches people's souls, warning them to change their ways. But they reject God, thinking that they can continue to do what they want. They decide not to repent until they can feel the coldness of eternity creep over their bodies. Even quite old people, to whom death is close, may take this attitude. God may touch them again and again, urging them to do good and avoid evil. And yet they resist God on every occasion, continuing to pursue material wealth and power. God may even cause them severe spiritual irritation by his persistence. But despite this irritation they seem to take a perverse delight in defying him. This seems especially strange in old people, who derive so little pleasure from sin.

— SC 3.8.8

When God touches evil people for the first time, they say to themselves: 'What is God to me? I don't want to have anything to do with his goodness.' They are so weighed down with their sins, and so confused by their own doubts, that they lack the mental energy to think about God. Then God touches them a second time. They may then feel less threatened by God's touch, because they have experienced it before. They say to themselves: 'I am not strong enough to change because my soul has been so weakened by sin.' They then enter a period of interior struggle in which the zeal that they once showed for sin is now transformed into a zeal for repentance. They become as busy in repenting for sin as they once were in committing sin. And gradually they wake up from the sleep of death, and embrace life. The sign that repentance is complete is that they no longer want to sin, in thought word or deed; they find sin as repulsive as they once found it attractive.

– SC 3.8.8

Sin is never a purely external act. Every sin which a person commits is swallowed by the soul, and the soul is polluted by it.

– SC 3.8.8

8

FEELINGS AND ATTITUDES

———————◆———————

People makes themselves weak and poor because they want to avoid working for justice and blotting out injustice. In short they do not want to pay back their debt to God. They prefer leisure to activity, and so fail to do the things which bring happiness. Others make themselves strong by running down the path that leads to truth. They make themselves rich in grace by drinking from the glorious fountain of God's Holy Spirit, and faithfully obeying the Spirit's instructions. These people enjoy great happiness, both on earth and in heaven.   – SC 1.1.6

There will be times in your life when you will murmur to yourself: 'The things that I achieve do not seem permanent, and they yield me no pleasure. I do not know whether I should find satisfaction, or whether my achievements are illusory.' The human mind is always prone to doubt. When people do good things, they are worried that God will not be pleased. And when people do bad things, they are terrified that God might not forgive them.

                                                    – SC 2.2.9

Trust yourself: trust your own will; and trust the devotion in your own soul.

— SC 2.5.39

Many become frustrated and bored with their work. Others come to regard it as beneath them, and feel humiliated. If you find yourself thinking in this way, do not imagine that you are the only one. Numerous people waver in their efforts. They continue working, but their hearts are no longer in what they do. They no longer look forward with clear eyes. And they do not seek the pure teaching which could resolve their predicament.

— SC 2.5.42

Just as God, from the abundance of his grace, pours out his blessings on all people, so you who have abundant wealth should share your material blessings with the poor. Just as Christ received people's help in order to serve them, so you who are poor should receive the gifts of others not out of greed, nor as an excuse for idleness, but as the means to work harder and more efficiently. There are many who prefer to be lazy; they refuse to do manual work in order to support themselves. These same people usually refuse to work spiritually also, in order to save their souls. They should not receive help, particularly if they have ignored those who encouraged them to mend their ways. But there are many others suffering physical need through no fault of their own, and who are devout in their prayers, working hard in spiritual ways for themselves and others. The rich who help such people receive back in spiritual blessings far more than they give materially.

– SC 2.6.91

Those who freely embrace poverty, in imitation of Christ and in the service of others, are greatly lovable to God. But those who are poor, and yet constantly hanker after wealth, are not cherished by God. Those who acquire riches in order to serve others more effectively are honoured by God. But those who acquire wealth in order to have power over others are like rotten carcasses to God.

— SC 2.6.92

Imagine an open market square, where the sinful delights of this world are for sale. The sellers do not appear evil; they are polite and gentle. There are three sorts of people in the square. The first are those who are dazzled by what they see, and eager to buy it; they willingly exchange their consciences for the sinful wares. The second are those who move quickly around the square, not buying anything; they clasp their consciences firmly, and refuse to exchange their consciences for anything. The third — the majority — saunter slowly through the market square, looking at everything for sale; they know that all the wares are sinful, but they allow themselves to be tempted by them — and they do not have the strength to resist.

— SC 2.7.4 and 5

Let people straighten their souls and bodies against evil. Let them inspect their own actions with a mixture of humility and fear. And when they realise that particular actions have been wrong, let them destroy the attitudes and intentions that led to those actions.

— SC 3.4.13

When people begin a good work, they are often uncertain and hesitant; they doubt whether their intentions are truly virtuous, and whether they possess the ability to complete the task. Thus they are vulnerable to evil influences pushing them off the path of virtue. In the middle of a good work they are usually more confident and courageous, and so cannot be deflected. Near the end fatigue and tiredness may make them vulnerable again. So be especially vigilant at the start and end of a good work.

— SC 3.4.13

Like all human beings, your inner sight is constantly changing. Sometimes you feel optimistic, sometimes angry, sometimes melancholy. Sometimes you look inside yourself, and see a happy person who enjoys life. Sometimes you are able to defy your own evil tendencies, and act with goodness and courage. Sometimes a terrible battle takes place inside you between your desire for good and the temptation towards evil. Sometimes you listen to God's guidance within your soul, and sometimes you are deaf to him.

— SC 3.5.3

When you perform a good work, you are afraid that it might not be perfect in the eyes of God. But this is because you do not know God clearly; you see him through darkened glass. Find God within yourself. Do not allow stupid emotions to obscure your awareness of his presence; and do not let your physical desires overwhelm your thoughts. When you discover God within yourself, you will be able to judge your own actions properly; you will know what actions conform to his will, and what actions are contrary to his will.

— SC 3.5.3

Many people are foolish. They do not wish to contemplate the enormity of God. They are frightened that an awareness of his enormity will strike terror into their hearts. Their greatest fear is fear. As a result they cannot be transformed by his goodness. They fail to discover God within themselves. They are like pirates plundering their own treasure.

— SC 3.5.7

9

MUSIC AND MEANING

Music is the echo of the glory and beauty of heaven. And in echoing that glory and beauty, it carries human praise back to heaven.

— SC 3.13.11

The words of a hymn represent the body, while the melody represents the soul. Words represent humanity, and melody represents divinity. Thus in a beautiful hymn, in which words and melody are perfectly matched, body and soul, humanity and divinity, are brought into unity.

— SC 3.13.12

Just as the power of God extends everywhere, surrounding all things and encountering no resistance, so too the sound of human voices singing God's praise can spread everywhere, surrounding all things and encountering no resistance. It can rouse the soul lost in apathy, and soften the soul hardened by pride.

— SC 3.13.13

In music you can hear the sound of burning passion in a virgin's breast. You can hear a twig coming into bud. You can hear the brightness of the spiritual light shining from heaven. You can hear the depth of thought of the prophets. You can hear the wisdom of the apostles spreading across the world. You can hear the blood pouring from the wounds of the martyrs. You can hear the innermost movements of a heart steeped in holiness. You can hear a young girl's joy at the beauty of God's earth. In music creation echoes back to its creator its joy and exultation; it offers thanks for its very existence. You can also hear in music the harmony between people who once were enemies and now are friends. Music expresses the unity of the world as God first made it, and the unity which is restored through repentance and reconciliation.   — SC 3.13.13

In musical harmony you hear the victory of the virtues, as they bring people together in love and charity. In musical disharmony you hear the skills of the devil, as he tries to divide people. In musical harmony you hear the virtues enabling people to overcome their faults, and to return to God in a spirit of repentance. In musical disharmony you hear harsh sourness which lies behind the gentle blandishments of the devil.   — SC 3.13.13

Musical harmony softens hard hearts. It induces in them the moisture of reconciliation, and it invokes the Holy Spirit. When different voices sing in unity, they symbolise the simple tenderness of mutual love. When different voices blend in song, they symbolise the blending of thoughts and feelings which is the highest pleasure human beings can know. Let the sweet sound of music enter your breast, and let it speak to your heart. It will drive out all darkness, and spread spiritual light to every part of you.

— SC 3.13.4

Never cease to praise God in song, Only through music can you truly express your devotion for him.

— SC 3.13.15

You who know, love and adore God, with simple and pure devotion, praise him with the sound of a trumpet – that is, with the faculty of reason ...

And praise him with the lyre of profound emotion, and with the harp of softness and gentleness.

And praise him with the timbrel of mortification and with the dance of exultation ...

And praise him with the strings of repentance, and with the organ of divine guidance ...

Praise him also with cymbals of true joy.

— SC 13.13.16

10

DREAMS AND EMOTIONS

———◆———

Just as the sun is the light of the day, so the soul is the light of the body – when it is awake. And just as the moon is the light of the night, so the soul is the light of the body – when it is asleep. When the body of a sleeping person has the right degree of warmth, then its marrow will also be warm to the right degree. When the soul of the sleeping person is free from the storm of conflict and immorality, dreams will often reveal the truth with great clarity; a restful soul has great power of discernment. In the same way the light of the moon shines bright and clear, when the night is free from storms and winds. But when the body and soul are beset, during the waking hours, with a storm of conflicting ideas and desires, that storm will persist during the night. And the soul will no longer have truthful dreams, but false ones. The soul is so darkened by these conflicts that it cannot see the truth – just as the moon cannot shine clearly when storm-clouds fill the sky.

– CC 83, 27

The soul is much weakened by evil dreams – by dreams which are morally and spiritually dark. The soul loses its clear vision, and becomes greatly deluded. If you allow negative thoughts into your mind, these will begin to terrorise the soul. The soul will be beset by false perceptions and by lies. Even the most holy people can be attacked by evil dreams, if they give way to negative thoughts.

– CC 83, 32

The soul, when dreaming, is burdened by the thoughts, opinions and emotions that preoccupy the waking mind. These thoughts, opinions and emotions are like the yeast within the dreams. If they are good, the dreams will be good; if they are bad, the dreams will be bad.

– CC 82, 32

If a person falls asleep with the mind occupied with evil desires, with anger or fear, with lust for power, and the like, then the devil will use all these in that person's dreams.

– CC 82, 33

The soul of a sleeping person can have many prophetic dreams, if that soul is not burdened with sin.

– CC 83, 22

11

VIRTUES: A DRAMA

The Virtues speak: 'We live in God and remain in God. We are soldiers in the army of the King of kings, and we overcome evil with good. We are visible in every good action ... and we come to the aid of all who call on us.'

The Souls placed in bodies complain: 'We are strangers. What have we done to deserve this fate? Why have we been cast into this prison? We are daughters of the King, and yet we live in this darkness. Living sun, carry us on your shoulders into our rightful inheritance.'

The Faithful Soul speaks: 'Sweet God, most blessed source of life, I forfeited the first bright garment which you gave me through my disobedience. Let me wear a second bright garment, and live among the Virtues.'

The Virtues answer: 'Happy Soul, sweet daughter of God, you have been nurtured in the wisdom of God, and have drunk his love from your mother's breast.'

The Faithful Soul responds: 'Freely I will come to you in order that I may receive your kiss.'

The Virtues say: 'We ought to serve as soldiers with you, daughter of the King.'

The Burdened Soul complains: 'The garment that I wear in this life – the body in which I find myself – is extremely heavy; and for me the slightest movement is hard.'

The Virtues answer: 'Burdened soul, you were created by God to be his blessed instrument. Why are you so weak against this body, which God also created? You have the strength to overcome its evil tendencies.'

The Burdened Soul cries out: 'Come quickly to my rescue, so that I can stand upright and move.'

Knowledge of God speaks to the Burdened Soul: 'Look carefully at your garment, and understand how it has been made. Then you will grow in strength.'

The Burdened Soul again cries out: 'I do not know what to do or where I might flee. I am not able to improve this body in which I am clothed. I want to throw it away.'

The Virtues respond: 'Unhappy soul, why do you turn your face against your creator?'

The Knowledge of God responds: 'Do you not see that the One who created you also created the body?'

The Burdened Soul replies: 'I understand that

God created the world, including this body. I do not wish the world any harm; I want to be at peace with the world.'

The Devil speaks to the Burdened Soul: 'You are right not to wish the world any harm. You should serve the world, and the world will give you great honour and pleasure.'

The Virtues cry out: 'We weep and wail because a soul is under threat.'

Humility, the queen of Virtues, speaks: 'Come to me, all you Virtues. I will nourish you, that you may persevere to the end.'

The Virtues respond: 'Our glorious queen, we come to you with joy.'

Humility continues: 'I will welcome you into my royal bedchamber, as my most beloved daughters. I am like a tree, and you are my branches.'

The Devil speaks to Humility and the other Virtues: 'Submit to my will, and you shall have count-less followers. With me you shall learn the full extent of your power and influence, and thus give much more to the world.'

Humility answers: 'I and my companions know who you are, and that you dwell in the lowest place in the universe.'

The Virtues add: 'We live in the highest place.'

The Burdened Soul repents: 'You, dear Virtues, are so beautiful and so sweet, and you bring such joy to those who embrace you, that I am ashamed of fleeing from you.'

The Virtues reply: 'Stop fleeing from us, and instead run towards us. Not only shall we receive you, but so also will God.'

The Burdened Soul continues: 'I am both attracted to you, dear Virtues, and also frightened of you. And I am still attached to the fiery sweetness of sin.'

The Virtues offer encouragement: 'Do not be anxious or frightened. We shall welcome you as a lost brother returning home.'

The Burdened Soul adds: 'The wounds which sin has inflicted on me fester. I need to be nursed and made well.'

The Virtues say: 'Come to us quickly. God will take care of you, healing your wounds; and we shall be the instruments of his love.'

The Burdened Soul says: 'I cannot believe that you want one so disgusting as me. My wounds and sores stink.'

The Virtues repeat their assurance: 'We welcome you as you are. Come quickly.'

The Burdened Soul relents: 'You are like a royal army dressed in white robes of peace. I come to you as a foreigner, begging your mercy. Help me to become a worthy friend. Heal me with the medicine of humility, because pride is the cause of my wounds. I run to you; receive me.'

Humility speaks to the Virtues: 'Receive this wounded soul, and lead her to me.'

The Virtues speak to the Burdened Soul: 'We will joyfully lead you, and we will never forsake you. All the heavenly army rejoices for you, and we sing in your honour.'

The Devil now speaks to the Burdened Soul: 'Who are you, and where do you come from? You embraced me and asked me to lead you; but now you turn your back and defy me. I will attack you and hurl you down.'

The Burdened Soul answers the Devil: 'From the start I knew your ways to be evil. So once I had the courage and strength, I fled from you. If you come to attack me, I will fight against you.'

The Burdened Soul turns to Humility: 'Queen of Virtues, help me with your medicine.'

Humility speaks to the other Virtues: 'You have given the courage and strength to the Soul who now is free. Go quickly to the Devil who continues to threaten her, and bind him.'

The Virtues reply: 'We will conquer the lord of deceit and trickery. We shall form an army against him.'

The Virtues conclude with a song of praise: 'Praise to you, Christ, king of the angels. Praise to you for never abandoning even the most sinful of souls. Praise to you for shining so brightly in the midst of darkness. You are a fountain of fire, which pours the passion of heavenly love into repentant souls. You are a wind which blows all your children towards this celestial home which you have prepared for them.'

— SC 3.13.9

FURTHER READING

The most recent translations of both *Scivias* and *The Book of Divine Works* have been published by Bear and Co. An anthology of Hildegard's works, edited by Fiona Bowie and Oliver Davies, has been published by SPCK.

Abbreviations used to indicate sources

SC	*Scivias*
DW	*Book of Divine Works*
CC	*Causes and Cures*
P	*Physica*

PHILOSOPHERS OF THE SPIRIT

Also in this series

Kierkegaard

- Is truth objective?
- Can we make real moral choices, or are our choices pre-determined?
- Who are the true saints and heroes of this world?

Kierkegaard, the nineteenth-century Danish philosopher, is both one of the most difficult and one of the most attractive thinkers of the modern period. He is regarded as the founder of existentialism.

This selection of his works, together with an easily readable summary of the principles of his thought and an outline of his life, offers a straightforward introduction to his complex ideas.

PHILOSOPHERS OF THE SPIRIT

Also in this series

Pascal

Blaise Pascal, writing in the seventeenth century, was both scientist and philosopher. He found a way of combining rational and religious scepticism. In penetrating and often witty epigrams, he saw clearly the paradoxes and dilemmas of the human condition., and he concluded that gambling on faith was the only way of resolving them.

PHILOSOPHERS OF THE SPIRIT

Also in this series

Socrates

Socrates, the great teacher of ancient Athens, was a philosopher and a mystic – and a notorious de-bunker. He wrote nothing down, and our only reliable witness is the works of his disciple Plato. Condemned to death by his enemies, the account of his final hours is one of the highlights of classical literaure.